EX CATHEDRA

XXIII

PETER JOANNIDES

Printed in the United States of America
Corrected second printing, 2019

ISBN 978-0-9892536-6-6

www.PetroulisI@gmail.com

PREFACE

This book is the latest installment of my ongoing **Ex Cathedra** series that had its inception in my major work, ***Amán Amán!*** (Amazon, 2013), nearly 42 years ago.

All other **Ex Cathedras** (exclusive of **Ex Cathedras 1** through **8**, which are embedded in ***Amán Amán!*** itself) have now been gathered together into two published volumes, **Ex Cathedras (IX-XV)** and **More Ex Cathedras (XVI-XXII)**.

Peter Joannides

December 1, 2013

Ex Cathedra

23rd
Encyclical

von Herrn Doktor Professor Peter Joannides

1

I'm still trying to win the lottery, but that doesn't mean I'm not aware that I'm like those greyhounds chasing after the mechanical rabbit.

2

I've given up railing against "most unique," "very unique."

It seems to be a lost cause.

3

Animals can't help what they do.

As well as men.

(Except for saints.)

(If any.)

4

I love the smite of "Love at First Sight."

.

5

I used to walk through woods where there were bears, swim in depths where there were sharks, amble by neighborhoods where there were dogs, walk along avenues where there was traffic…

I don't do things like this anymore.

6

I've tried, I've tried! I've tried my best to get over this thing with accents.

But I can't help it.

I find myself saying, "Thank God, Thank God! I wasn't born into a family that talked like that."

7

Figs at their best: all soft and soggy and drippingly silken and sweet.

Ex Cathedra 21, # 167

I forgot Etō Jun of Tokyo, Japan.

9

Who could be a greater mongrel than a Cypriot?

Driving, driving, how many hours and hours of driving. Jacksonville and back and forth to Virginia, back and forth to St. Augustine, Daytona, Miami, hardly giving it a thought to shoot up to Asheville to see Michele and Wilmington to see Jack Morris and Raleigh to visit Bob Bryan, Jacksonville to Cincinnati and Cincinnati to Jacksonville, tournaments in Atlanta and Charlotte and Houston and even Vegas, in olden days back and forth from Virginia to New York, from Hampton to Williamsburg to Richmond to Charlottesville…

oh how many hours and hours, how much monolithic time spent encapsulated in an automobile.

11

I'm rapidly moving in the direction of forgiving everyone.

I'm absolutely on the side of blackjack card counters.

(If the casinos can't stand the heat, then let them get out of the game.)

13

I miss my family of old.

14

Dog-lovers and cat-lovers all over this planet: I love to stick it to them.

15

Ever "lost," "by the wind grieved," "lost," "on the edge of a grimpen," "in a dark wood," all along the way, not knowing, not understanding, ever in confusion, even now, ever bewildered in a fog and "lost."

16

What an all-embracing and succinct way of expressing the correct moral philosophy: to be pro-pleasure and anti-pain.

To say it again, in a little different way:

If Indian cuisine gets a 1, Indian music gets a 9.

18

All these primitive customs—these dances, costumes, colorful spectacles and rites—are beginning to wear thin.

19

I'm rapidly moving in the direction of forgiving everything.

20

MY Superlatives and Unsuperlatives

Most Beautiful Country: Morocco
Most Interesting Countries: Japan, Brazil; Least: Luxembourg
Most Likeable People: Italians; Least: Pashtuns
Most Exotic Countries: Haiti, Bangladesh
Most Soothing Language: Portuguese
Most Amazing Language: that of the Bushmen of the Kalahari
Best Dessert: crème caramel
Greatest Writer: Logan Pearsall Smith
Best Music: Andean, Greek; Worst: Modern jangly American

(continued)

21

Best Cuisine: Greek; Worst: Indian
Best Drivers: Englishmen; Worst: Spaniards, Jamaicans
Greatest Philosopher: F.W. Nietzsche
Greatest Sport: American handball; Worst: car racing
Greatest Poets: Thomas Wolfe, T. S. Eliot
Best President: FDR; Worst: Richard Nixon
Best Comedian: Sid Caesar; Worst: Milton Berle
Best Mystery Writer: Rex Stout

(continued)

Best Film: **Rashomon**; Worst: **Down Among the Sheltering Palms**
Best Porn: X½ – XX; Worst: XXXX
Sexiest Actress: Paulette Goddard
Greatest Avocation: travel
Best Drug: alcohol
Best Religion: Buddhism
Finest Fruit: mango

23

Maybe I wasn't as unobservant as I thought I was.

Ex Cathedra 18, # 3

George Tobias

It was **Juke Girl** that did it!

25

Oh if only if only I could undo and re-do all the witch hunts, wars, accidents, tragedies, illnesses, pains and sufferings…

Isn't this the ultimate science-fiction idea?

Hubert Horatio Humphrey

I remember him. Hardly paid any attention. I was busy with my life, and unpolitical, and in the back of my mind relegated that raspy voice and preachy intensity to another of those political hacks.

Now I learn about the things he tried to accomplish, the principles he stood for, the sort of man he was.

Now, so many years later, to suddenly realize that, what I thought to be a bombastic haranguer, was probably a very good and decent man.

27

There must be another way of choosing…no, not choosing…but of establishing, forming, of rising to the fore, a government.

28

Petros Epitropakis, Carlo Buti, Carlos Gardel, Tex Beneke, Sophia Vembo, Edith Piaf, Doris Day...

What a treasure trove of voices!

Objects, galaxies, electrons, humans, animals, reveries, dreams, abstractions, equations, pains, pleasures, hallucinations, mirages, moods, memories, ideas, images, pasts, futures, imaginations, spaces, numbers…

What do they all have in common?

30

You start a Third Party only if you have a reasonable chance of winning.

You don't spoil the chances for the better of the other two.

31

It's a little late for me to be so brave and courageous and to say this now, but I say it nonetheless (copy to: Alexander, Cyrus, Caesar, Napoleon, Tamerlane, Suleiman the Magnificent, Attila, Hitler, et al.):

To Politicos and Generals

I'll be goddamned if I'll be your little foot soldier and cannon fodder for all your Grand Designs and Grandiose Ambitions.

Go Fuck Yourself!

32

Oh if only I could travel about, and instantly, in some kind of impervious and plastic bubble, from which I can come and go as I please (with all the amenities I am used to), to Africa and the Middle East and Japan and Switzerland and Ceylon and Tahiti…

say, in the year 1874.

33

The littlest little pain looms large for me.

34

I love to peek into the intricate and silver diagrammatic innards of electronic products.

I love the thought of batteries: all that stored energy locked into minikin wafers and buttons and unassuming oblong tubes.

Oh if only I could travel about, and instantly, in some kind of impervious and plastic bubble, from which I can come and go as I please (with all the amenities I am used to), to places that surely will have changed in ways I cannot even begin to imagine...

say, in the year 2140.

It has turned out uncannily as predicted—modern cloverleafs and traffic arabesques.

And yet how profoundly unlike the wondrous faëryland of the 1939 General Motors Futurama.

38

So many of those Upper Echelon Republicans remind me of the **Invasion of the Body Snatchers**.

39

The order of languages in terms of Global Importance (as of September, 2012):

English, French, Spanish, Arabic, Chinese… OR   English, Spanish, French, Arabic, Chinese…

After that, it can go every which way.

(Of course, I am personally partial to Portuguese, Italian, and Turkish, but I can't let that interfere with Global Rankings.)

40

I don't imagine **Zarathustra's** "Old and Young Women" (First Part, 18) would sit too well with many old and young women these days.

41

No matter how smart one is (especially in his bailiwick and revered specialty), his opinions will invariably be uneven and often less than sterling, and sometimes downright fatuous and laughable.

42

I don't think I'd mind **painlessly** zapping thugs and hooligans.

MY priorities when reading the local paper:

lotto results
jumble puzzle
international news
political cartoons
local law and disorder
artsy stuff
----
local meetings and goings-on
obituaries
sports
business and finance

44

Innocent ones who have spent years and years in prison: this disturbs me **GREATLY**.

45

The thing about the lottery is that if ever you win the big one, you never have to buy another lottery ticket again.

You mustn't feel intimidated by all those speakers of mysterious foreign languages.

Most of what is being said is probably as pedestrian and inane as what you hear in English.

47

No matter what personal upheavals, epiphanies, vicissitudes, embarkations may take hold, the weave and line of traffic—the intersections, red lights, delays, back-ups—remain (like "Ol' Man River") ever the same.

Professor Alvin Plantinga

What a lot of orotund nonsense.

(There's something about apologists who want to have it both ways and even three or four ways ((and just can't **let go**)), and skeptics who can't take their skepticism straight, that really does irritate...and sadden.)

49

I can never forget the dance of the tall Watusi in **King Solomon's Mines**.

To this day when idly finger-strumming on whatever surface there may happen to be, I invariably strum to the cadence of that remarkable dance.

50

I no doubt have an oversized ego, but oh how droopy and deflated it gets when confronted with the wonders and intricacies of technology.

51

What is going on? Practically every time I get into the car to go from one local spot to another, I find myself lapsing into a kind of Sid Caesar-like parody of nonsense German. I go along with it, amusing and diverting as it is. But it keeps happening all the time. What is going on?!

While some are dying in hospitals, burning to death, drowning, having their homes smashed to bits by a tornado, involved in gruesome road accidents, stabbed, murdered, festering in hunger, disease, and pain…

Others are taking cruises, acting out comic routines, going to proms, cheering football teams, being picky about their wardrobes, tending to a minor fender bender of their cars, doing crossword puzzles…

53

I envy the **money** of celebrities.

That's about it.

I envy the **money** of CEO's, hedge fund managers, entrepreneurs, politicos, college presidents, gangsters, drug lords…

That's about it again.

55

It's been many a Rhodian year,

Since I've had a retsina from CAIR.

56

Unless you write it down, many an extraordinary thought will fly away,

And not come back for many a day.

57

Monolinguists are blissfully unaware,

Of whole other worlds and ken (right under their noses) coexisting out there.

When Academic Brahmins sometimes declare a phraseology to be grammatically wrong, I say "Right On!"

And other times, I say "Pedantry!"

What sort of self-respecting individual would allow himself to be interviewed on the back end of a national magazine with a series of quick-fire and imbecilic, impertinent, drooly personal questions—who is the greatest love of your life? who is your favorite writer? what is the trait you most deplore in yourself? what is your idea of perfect happiness?...

The sad part is that not only publicity-lapping hounds take part, but also actors, celebrities, politicos, judges, even intellectuals and scientists for whom I have a certain amount of half-respect.

(continued)

There hardly seems a one who isn't a potential participant.

I now wait for the President and the Queen of England to take their turn.

All and everyone in the common, mismashed, collective slime together.

61

Why do so many American Jews go so out of
their way to let you know they're Jewish?

I know of no other people, ethnic nationalities,
who do this.

"Daybreak" by Maxfield Parrish

Force Fields are in place.

Noiseless, unobtrusive, invisible.

Butterflies, dragonflies, hummingbirds come through.

Flies, mosquitoes, wasps, gnats, ticks, chiggers are kept at bay.

63

Maxfield Parrish

Repin

Velázquez

That's about it.

I seem to now be discarding former selves—
quicker and quicker, one right after another.

My favorite of Logan Pearsall Smith's crystalline **Trivia** gems is the one in which he, the craven white-livered milksop, hasn't the guts to eat the plovers' eggs meant for poor Gertrude.

I'm fascinated by the thought of a Morse code being transmitted in the middle of a tropical jungle.

The individual sounds would be intrinsically similar to their surrounding cacophony.

But what a world of difference in the structure and pattern!

Can we apply this analogy to language, and to **certain** writers and their **certain** audience?

67

Mitt Romney

See Ex Cathedra 21, # 23

How fortunate we are to be living in this day and age: not having to smell horse manure all the time, air conditioning, **anaesthesia**, sewage disposal, curtailment of disease, television, Google, DVD's, remotes, morphine, international cuisine at our fingertips, air travel, internet, instant heating, communications…

I wonder what they'll be saying in 2140.

(If anyone's around in 2140.)

69

I hated Bette Davis as a kid; I adored her as an adult.

70

Some other actors I hated as a kid:

Lynn Bari

Victor Mature

Joan Crawford

Alexis Smith

71

Mitt Romney

What was it that the Injuns would say in old Westerns of yesteryear:

"Him speak with forked tongue."

72

I **DETEST** graffiti.

Of any sort.

I love the way a train **S-L-I-C-E-S** through things.

(Culverts, embankments, buildings, stopped cars, barred roadways, streams, tunnels, bulwarks, forests, bridges, zip, zip, zip—all obeisant, arrested, giving way.)

(All melting, opening, not a one daring to obstruct the sovereign and lordly train.)

Daydream 1

The Day the Earth Stood Still

Aliens arrive and invest me with power over several Gorts with their deathly visor rays. I plant one in Washington, one in Beijing, one in Brussels, one in Moscow, one in Cairo, one in Brasilia, and one in Jakarta.

Henceforth, all to know there is to be a new Boss running things.

Daydream 2

Arthur C. Clark's **Childhood's End**.

With the help of aliens, copies of **Childhood's End** mysteriously appear in the personal bedrooms of Barack Obama, José Barroso, Hu Jintao, Vladimir Putin, Manmohan Singh, Ban Ki-moon…(translated into Portuguese, Chinese, Russian, Hindi, and Korean respectively…) with especial notation of the pages describing the "silent shadows driving across the stars" and the large bipeds with leathery wings, horns, and tails.

Henceforth, all to know there is to be a new Boss running things.

Georges Simenon

A writer who could turn out a novel of quality in two weeks, who is read and acclaimed by millions, and who has the respect and imprimatur of the severest critics.

A total success.

Ex Cathedra 22, # 154

I forgot all about bamboo.

What is that line of T.S. Eliot— "…humility is endless."

79

There is nothing wrong with growing old so long as one has his "f-a-c-u-l-t-i-e-s intact" and hasn't any pain or nausea or dizziness or restriction of movement.

A waiter (waitress) with a sunny disposition—it makes all the difference in the world.

Mitt Romney

It's all about ambition, and nothing else.

82

Mitt Romney

I even liked Nixon better.

83

When two speak not the same language, no matter in how many other ways they tally and accord, it's still a comedy of errors.

I absolutely **gobbled up** these writers: Jules
Verne, Thomas Wolfe, Logan Pearsall Smith, Rex Stout.

85

Arab garb **in the States** irritates me no end.

86

It's still mystifying to me how a remote can open up a heavy metal gate.

Every day new things swim into view—writers, practices, procedures, pundits, celebrities, customs, histories, locations, words, workings—that I had no idea about the day before.

Alexander, **THE GREAT**

A carousing, adolescent stripling of thirty-three.

Give me a break.

All my so beautiful girlfriends—Helen, Aida, Fujiko, Rattayaporn, Marlena, Ursula—now either dead, or soon to be elderly ladies.

90

I wonder if I should have spent all those not so
unsizable chunks of time learning languages,

Instead of playing handball.

I have my problems with physicists; but, then again, I can't very well argue with the atomic bomb.

November 7, 2012

…, despite all the nerds, cornballs, rednecks, religious nuts, dolts, featherbrains, pathetic patriots… who voted.

93

I've said it before, and I say it again:

There is hardly a sound more irritating than that of a bouncing basketball.

94

I remember words of long ago: "You have the shoulder of an 80-yr-old man," "He shuffles around like an 80-yr-old man," "An 80-yr-old stoop," "An octogenarian"…

And now (how did it happen?) here I really am.

More and more evanescent whiffs of bygone days, hardly identifiable, hardly describable: somewhere, a shaft of sunlight; somewhere, I know not where, a morning crispness; a fragrance; a sudden elation; a remembrance of a kindness; an old and pregnant fig tree; a summer pathway; an elusive and teasing hint of some half-forgotten purple flower.

96

I know of no truer, better, more earnest and poignant title than "You Can't Go Home Again."

I bet, if I wanted to, I could learn the intricacies of an iPhone in a couple of weeks, maybe a month, maybe two. I just don't have the desire or energy to do so.

98

I like to listen to Frank Deford, even though I hardly know what he's talking about.

99

All my life I've been waiting for the telephone call that never came.

When confronted with engineers, mechanics, scientists (e.g., those responsible for getting "Curiosity" to Mars)…and to a lesser extent economists, mathematicians, statisticians…I feel so intimidated, ignorant, unworthy, presumptuous…

And yet maybe what I have done and do also has an important place in the general scheme of things.

101

There are lots of androgynes in the News business.

102

I don't know what makes people think we're so terribly different from other animals.

103

Sometimes I think that eventually all of our most private moments, our casual conversations, self-musings, exclamations—perhaps even **past** ones—will be open and available for public inspection and scrutiny.

One of the wonders of this world: how a skin wound slowly, and step by step, and bit by bit, and layer upon layer, methodically heals itself.

105

Yappy little dogs: how I wish I could incinerate them.

106

I wouldn't want to inflict pain, however, even on yappy little dogs.

107

Senator Lindsey Graham of South Carolina

All I have to do is listen to that drawl, and I know what he's all about.

Confession

F. Nietzsche: I've only read **Zarathustra** and not much more.

Logan Pearsall Smith: I've only read **All Trivia** and not much more.

T.S. Eliot: I've only read **Prufrock** and **Four Quartets** and not much more.

Why would anybody want to play:

Sherlock Holmes, after Basil Rathbone;

Tarzan, after Johnny Weissmuller;

James Bond, after Sean Connery.

When I become Planetary Dictator, I will round up and expropriate all the great chefs of this world.

111

I wonder if everyone does this: tells the same old stories over and over and over again.

112

It's hard to escape the thought: that from an astronomic point of view, everything we do is sort of pointless.

I, who as a kid loved to play cops and robbers, detectives, master spy, secret agent, who loved gats and guns, held them close to my breast and in the holster by my side, loved the make-believe of zinging bullets, the twiiing of near-misses, out to get the evil-doers, save the day...

I, now detest the very sight of guns, hate the very look and sheen of guns, hate all the gun-lovers and the gun shops and the lethal array of all their disgusting wares, hate the target practicers and the apologists and the sleazy self-righteous 2nd Amendment defenders and everything and anything to do with these ugly and evil and immoral atrocities.

114

Some of the opinions of my friends are quite terrible.

But my friends still remain my friends, notwithstanding.

When I read a newspaper, I steer way clear of opinions, and hone right in on facts.

For a writer, there is such a thing as a factual typo.

I agree with James Jones: Thomas Wolfe is a greater writer than William Shakespeare.

Of all the places in my travels, the only one where it crossed my mind that I could actually move there and live there: Trento, Italy.

119

For me, child-actors have nearly always been a disaster.

It's remarkable how a substantial sample of traveling can stand the stead of just about all of traveling.

121

It's amazing how some orators can be so eloquent, grandiloquent, with an unbelievable command of language and gesture and pause and crescendo…

and still be retarded.

Oh, could I give any number of examples!

122

The "media" love to focus on a media tragedy for days and days on end, giving every bit of illumination and every minute detail, over and over again, and once more again...

Notwithstanding that equal tragedies happen all the time, to so many people, all over the place.

123

Writing for money is an abomination.

What is this "No one should be above the law"?

The Dictator is above the law.

The Dictator **makes** the law.

125

There is no way I can tell the story of Dostoyevsky's "Peasant Marey" without breaking up.

(I owe this blubbering embarrassment and yet precious legacy to my friend and University of Virginia classmate Bob Strong, who then went on to study Russian language and literature.)

126

The science-fiction writers were always way ahead of everybody else.

127

The most cheerful of the Greek islands: Kos.

There's something really beautiful about a $100 bill.

129

I love to have a drink when driving.

Not long ago I said that there's a lot to like about Christopher Hitchens, and I stand by it, but that pervasive **intensity** sometimes does discomfit me.

131

I no longer drive on icy roads.

132

Every time I reread my work, I am reminded of the words of Swift:

"What genius I had then!"

133

Changing the pitch and inflection of the voice:

All **speeches** are more or less ridiculous.

134

I am getting older and older, and I just realized that I like, and always have, the Currier and Ives Christmas prints.

135

Senator Cornyn of Texas: another Republican asshole.

Handball

In my prime (**Masters** and **Golden Masters**), I was somewhere between an A player and an AA player.

For a few heady moments, I entered the rarefied realm of an AAA player.

I'm beginning to realize that so many of my **Ex Cathedra** entries are simply **extensions** of the Magnum Opus—extensions, re-statements, recapitulations, repetitions.

Maybe it's time for Steve Inskeep of NPR to retire, or perhaps find some other outlet for his sunny and hearty and chummy logorrhea.

139

So many crosses to bear…

For so many…

140

Somehow, I've gone through life without getting on a cruise ship.

Now, I've come out the other end and have no desire to get on a cruise ship.

141

There **are** good doctors.

There **are** good surgeons.

142

After I assume the Dictatorship, when it comes to my attention that someone is a torturer, and it is established beyond a reasonable doubt that this is so, that individual will be, not tortured, but immediately and totally extinguished.

143

Fiction that mimics **REAL** events is nearly always a turn-off.

144

No matter what edibles and comestibles are there for the asking, I can't seem to get enough of my fill of **BREAD**.

145

"There are more things in heaven and earth, Horatio,

Than are dreamt of in your philosophy."

Surely, this has to be one of the wisest lines of all literature.

Some of the women on the covers of old Sci-Fi magazines were quite sexy.

147

My friend Walter Bass:　didn't realize what a lacuna he left in my life, until he was gone.

It's hard to think of a white-collar job worse than being a Superintendent of Schools.

I would think it'd be a job that could easily drive one to suicide.

149

Sarah Palin

A sick lady. Not quite as sick as Ann Coulter, but sick nonetheless.

How obsolete the Computer and Internet have
made all my IBM Selectric clickety-clackings and
library rummagings researchings and wormy persevering
sleuthings!

A surreal expectation that I have no way of understanding or explaining:

A mesh of times—early childhood, the music and ambience of the 20's, the present accomplishment in literature and philosophy, that long-ago day with mama on the steps of Columbia University—all dovetailing into one another and strangely simultaneous—and included, invariably, the tuxedoed and lively-mannered and boutonniered Franchot Tone.

Every time a Democrat appears on television, I feel a certain perfusing gladness.

I must take back something I wrote many many years ago:

That a roast kid can never measure up to a roast lamb.

That was a mistake. It all depends upon who is doing the preparing, and where.

Anyone who has had a melting-in-your-mouth kid at Psinthos and Efta Piyes in Rhodos knows that this is not true.

151

It's as if I will suddenly come upon a ME of long ago, ME as a child (of promise), and **at the same time** a ME as an adult (in the company of and carousing with Franchot Tone), but a different ME from the ME of now (and looking on approvingly), and yet **at the same time** the ME to be the ME of now.

.

155

I wouldn't mind spending a few days at the Coco Point Lodge in Barbuda.

Many of my comments, unflattering remarks, barbs, skewerings were written right off the top of my head.

157

I'm not as tough as I thought I was.

158

I wish Piers Morgan would go back to the U.K.

159

I don't think I would have liked Isaiah Berlin.

I really have no good reason for saying this.

But there it is.

Senator Marco Rubio

A Latino pipsqueak, dripping with ambition.

"Man's Inhumanity to Man"

I've been hearing this phrase for years—sort of half-understanding and half-registering it.

Now, I know only too well what it means.

Sadly, it has taken this long.

162

There was once a Mafia don called John,

Whose other name I won't let on.

I sometimes wonder: Was there any saving grace whatever,

To one so steeped in mayhem, malice, and murder?

163

I hate this summer weather—this hell—in Jacksonville.

I hate it with a passion.

164

When there is mango in the offing, I cannot wait around for it to fit into some culinary schedule.

I want it **NOW**.

Here I am, half a geographical man, half an electronic man.

166

Chocolate pudding without whipped cream: a lamentation.

Fags shouldn't be involved in literary criticism. (John Horne Burns.)

An attack on Wolfe is an attack on me.

168

I wonder: Are there blind people in Bhutan? And paralytics, psychotics, amputees, dementia sufferers, dwarfs?

169

Big misunderstandings are often tied to quite little slips and missteps.

Dessert should be had **with** a meal, not **after** a meal.

171

The Buddha

I wonder if electrodes were strapped to his body
causing excruciating pain most, if not all, of the time…

I wonder what serenity he would have found.

Freud had it all pretentiously wrong about dreams.

Dreams are so surreal, they outsurreal the surreal. Locations magically change places, individuals quickly meld into different individuals, times become interchangeable, forever elusive levels of awareness that flit and coalesce and diverge…

When dreams are **described** and focused on, they become **flattened** and **unidimensionalized,** and thus hardly true, and lost.

Dreams should just be experienced, and left at that.

Etymology surely has to be one of the most ego-deflating disciplines.

.

How about Wendy Davis for higher office!

175

A retarded and handicapped child: nothing tears
my guts out more than this.

176

All these varying perspectives conspire to suck me in. And for a while I do get sucked in. But in the end I refuse to get sucked in. And I come back out to myself...and to **my** perspective.

177

Those who give speeches and talks to **large** numbers of people are nothing less than embarrassing and pitiful.

All this talk about money—debentures, IRA's, 401K's, interest rates, DOW, NASDAQ, S&P, hedge funds, insider tradings, mutual funds, stock market quotes, portfolios, bonds, collaterals—bores me to tears.

I just want to have a lot of it to **SPEND**.

I wonder how many people can spell "Houyhnhnms" correctly.

180

I'd rather not hear Thomas Wolfe's voice.

I believe I said that the optimum population for this planet would be 300,000,000.

I hereby now revise it down to 100,000,000.

Philosophers should no longer be talking about God; only historians.

Actors emoting and mouthing off in ads, makes me want to throw up.

184

Aside from the content of what was said, about which I know little, I found Charlie Rose's interview with Bashar al-Assad nothing less than **embarrassing**, even as I did that idiot President of Columbia University inviting Ahmadinejad to New York and then insulting him up, down, and sideways.

185

All along the way,

    I never knew then, what I came to know after.

Neil deGrasse Tyson

A bit of a showman, but still quite likeable.

187

Another big embarrassment: watching those who actually **enjoy** teaching and directing others.

188

Senator Ted Cruz of Texas: and yet another Republican asshole.

189

Clumsily attempting to break two fused ice cubes apart, I drew blood from one of my fingers.

Ice is definitely a solid.

(The thought of the **Titanic** flashed through my mind.)

I wish I could speak Greek as well as Evangelos Venizelos.

Of all the Bing Crosby - Bob Hope - Dorothy Lamour **Road** pictures, **Road to Morocco** was the best.

192

I'm all for Senator Barbara Mikulski!

193

A question/answer interview should always be preceded by this:

I may not be able to answer your question.

I may not want to answer your question.

If I can answer and want to answer, I'll do my best to do so.

194

Anyone who would characterize me as a kind of homologue of Don Quijote tilting at windmills, would not be very far off the mark.

What a **SET UP!** Animals killing other animals. Proteins ingesting proteins. Pain, fear, struggle, predation, death. (Even among plants—the strangler vines, and the travail in the jungle canopy.)

Couldn't there have been another sort of blueprint?

City for Conquest is a special movie for me. It
is a long-ago bond between my father and myself.

What if one should suddenly realize that, after years and years of mouthing off on all sorts of subjects, he really had no idea of what he was talking about.

Professor Niall Ferguson

Something's not quite right here, but I can't put my finger on what it is.

199

Football, boxing, car racing: to be immediately outlawed as soon as I assume the Dictatorship.

Cialis ads: I don't know which adjective to use—sickening, disgusting, stomach-turning, nauseating.

www.ingramcontent.com/pod-product-compliance
Lightning Source LLC
Chambersburg PA
CBHW071959040426
42447CB00009B/1405